WITHDRAWN

S0-ATE-455

EL DORADO COUNTY LIBRARY
345 FAIR LANE
PLACERVILLE, CA 95667

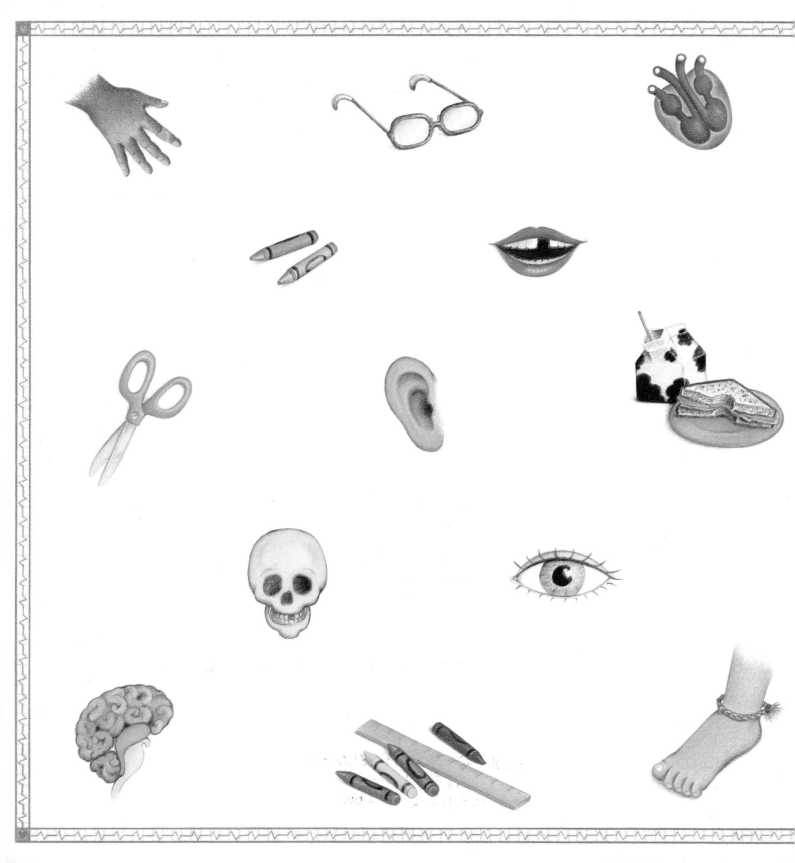

ME AND MY
AMAZING BODY

by Joan Sweeney   illustrated by Annette Cable

Crown Publishers, Inc. 👑 New York

EL DORADO COUNTY LIBRARY
345 FAIR LANE
PLACERVILLE, CA 95667

For my amazing son, John, the doctor
—J.S.

To all children—take care of and be happy with your bodies.
This is your gift to yourself.
—A.C.

Text copyright © 1999 by Joan Sweeney
Illustrations copyright © 1999 by Annette Cable
All rights reserved. No part of this book may be reproduced or transmitted
in any form or by any means, electronic or mechanical, including photocopying,
recording, or by any information storage and retrieval system,
without permission in writing from the publisher.

Published by Crown Publishers, Inc., a Random House company,
201 East 50th Street, New York, NY 10022

CROWN is a trademark of Crown Publishers, Inc.

www.randomhouse.com/kids

Printed in Singapore

Library of Congress Cataloging-in-Publication Data
Sweeney, Joan, 1930-
Me and my amazing body / by Joan Sweeney ; illustrated by Annette Cable. —1st ed.
p. cm.
Summary: A girl describes how her skin, bones, muscles, brain, blood, heart, lungs,
and stomach receive energy and function as parts of her body.
1. Human anatomy—Juvenile literature. [1. Human anatomy.
2. Human physiology. 3. Body, Human.] I. Cable, Annette, ill. II. Title.
QM27.S94 1999
[611]—dc21 98-34628

ISBN 0-517-80053-5 (trade)
0-517-80054-3 (lib. bdg.)

10 9 8 7 6 5 4 3 2 1

First Edition

This is me and my amazing body.

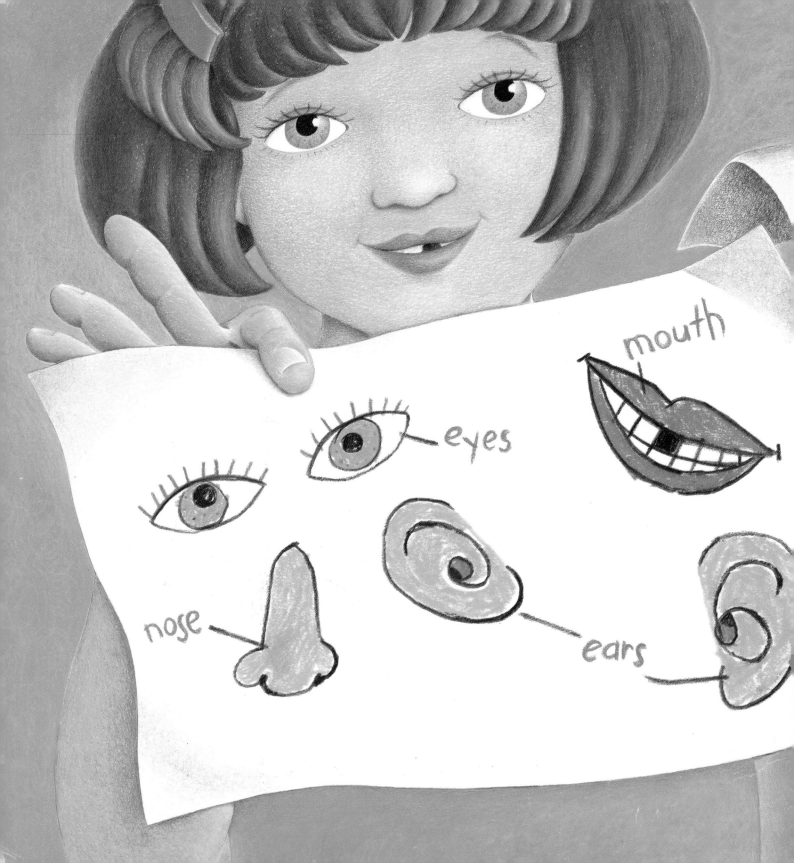

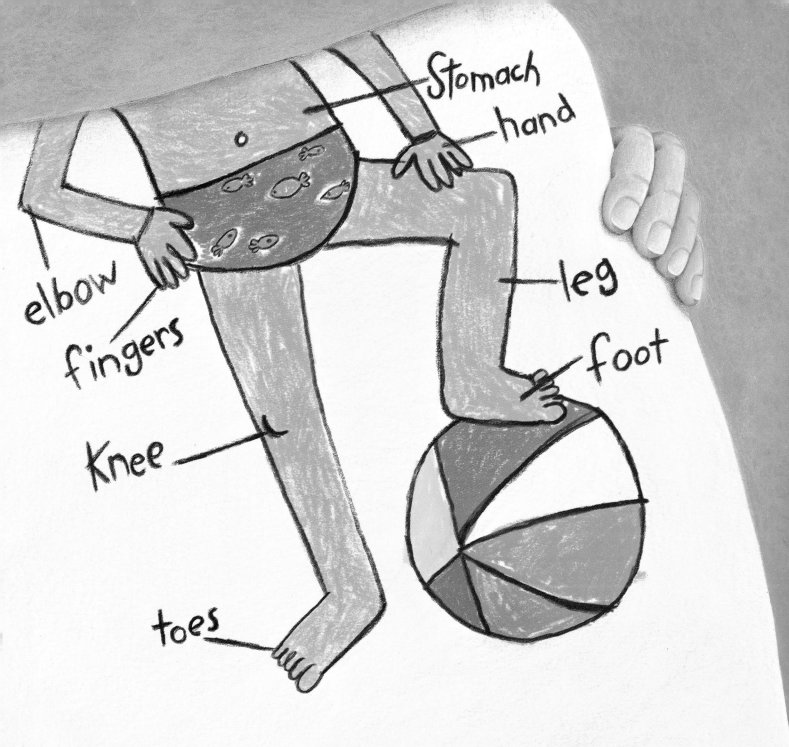

These are the parts of my body that I can see.

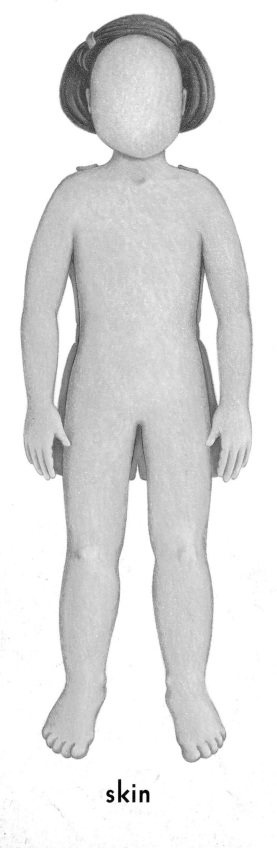

skin

But most of my body I *can't* see, because my **skin** covers almost every inch of it. Skin comes in many different colors. It holds my body together and lets me feel things, like my kitty's soft fur or the prickly spikes of my cactus. Ouch!

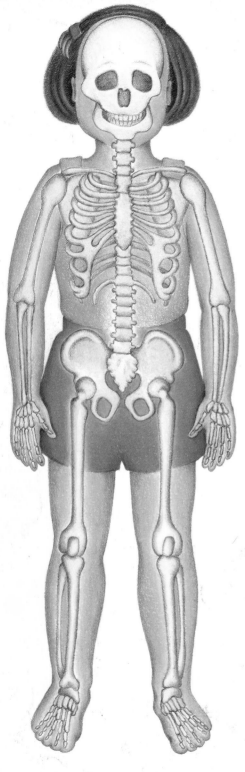

bones

Beneath my skin are my **bones**. All 206 of them! When my bones are put together, they're called a skeleton. My skeleton holds up my skin, just like tent poles hold up a tent. Bones are hard and help protect the softer insides of my body.

Attached to my bones are my **muscles**.
My body has more than 600! They
stretch and shrink like rubber bands.
Muscles do the hard work of moving
my body all around, back and forth,
and up and down. I even use my
muscles when I smile!

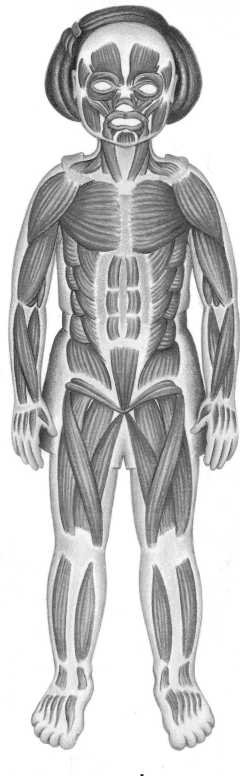

muscles

My muscles move because my **brain** tells them to. My brain is the boss of my body, and it lets me think my own special thoughts. It's so important that it has its own safe place in my head—inside a very hard bone called my skull. My brain sends and receives messages from all parts of my body.

mouth

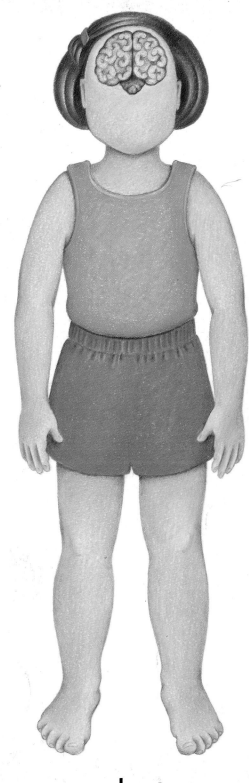

brain

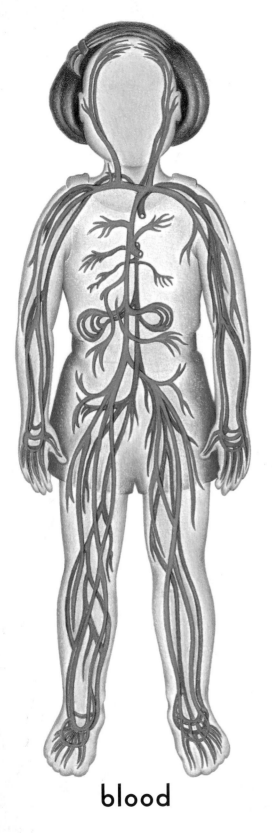

blood

My body and my brain need lots of energy to work well. They get energy from my **blood**. Blood contains oxygen from the air and nourishment from the food that I eat. My blood travels all over my body through special tubes called veins and arteries. If I cut or scrape my skin and it bleeds, don't worry! My body is always making more blood.

My blood can't move through my body all by itself. It needs my **heart**— a group of strong muscles in my chest—to move it. My heart is like my own little engine. It pumps blood through my body all the time, even when I'm sleeping! If I put my hand on my chest, I can feel my heart beating.

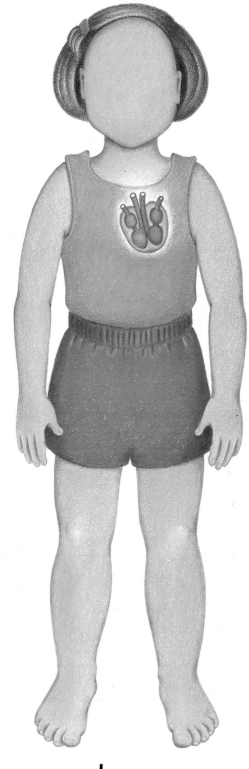

heart

I can also feel my **lungs** working when I breathe in deep. My lungs fill with fresh air like balloons and send the part of the air that I need—the oxygen—into my blood.

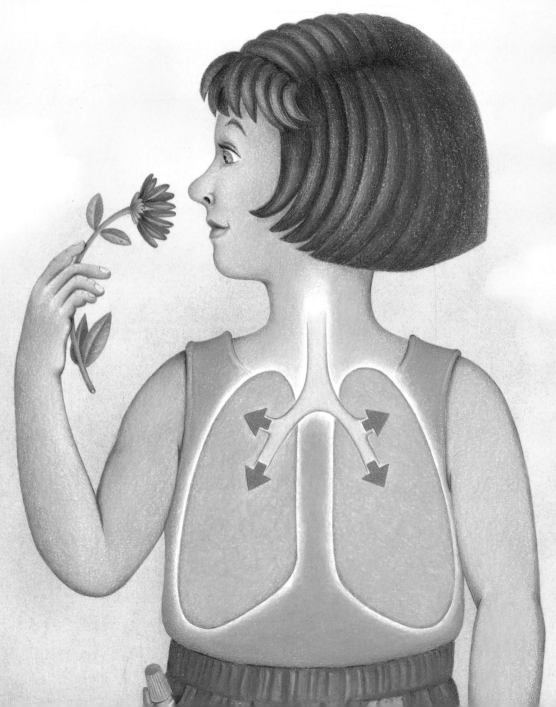

Then my lungs push the used air back out. A moment later, I breathe in fresh air all over again.

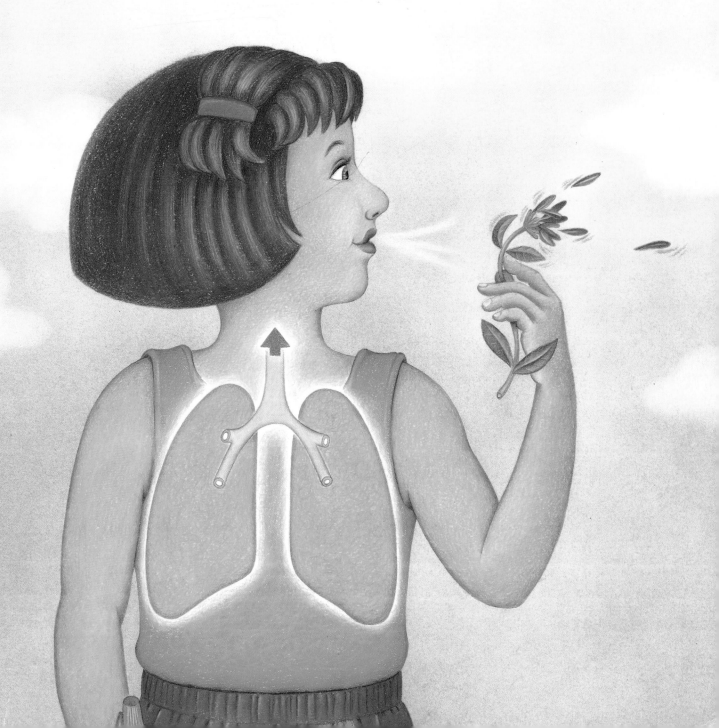

My body needs food along with air—or else I wouldn't grow!
When I get hungry I eat, and the food goes down into my
stomach. After I eat, my stomach mashes the food into
very tiny pieces. Then my body takes what it needs for
energy and growth, and gets rid of whatever it doesn't need.

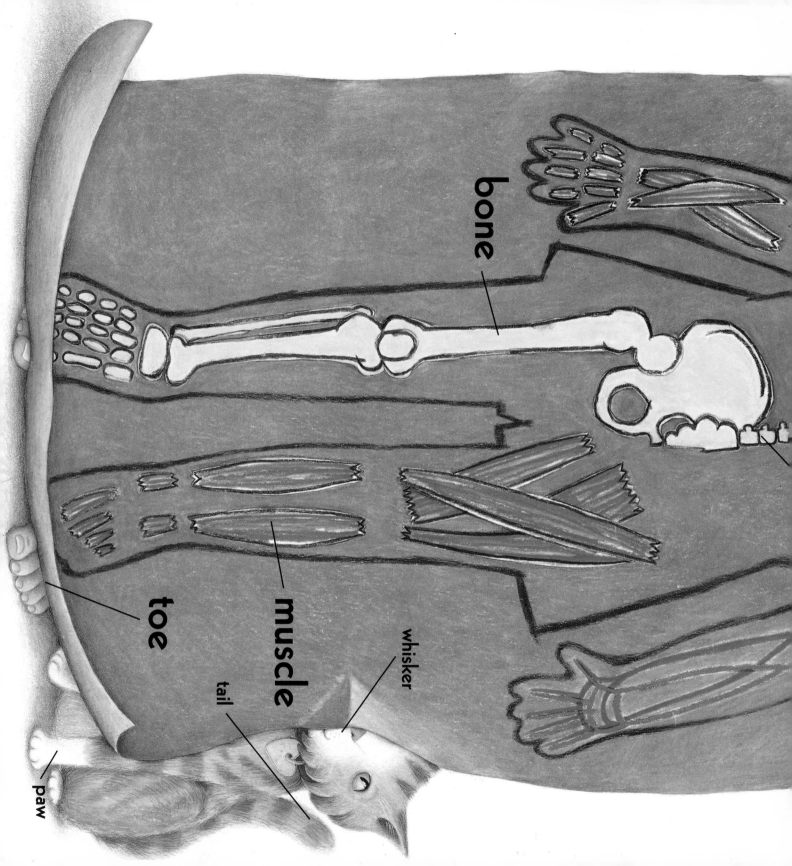

bone

toe

muscle

tail

whisker

paw

Every part of my body works together to keep me going . . . .

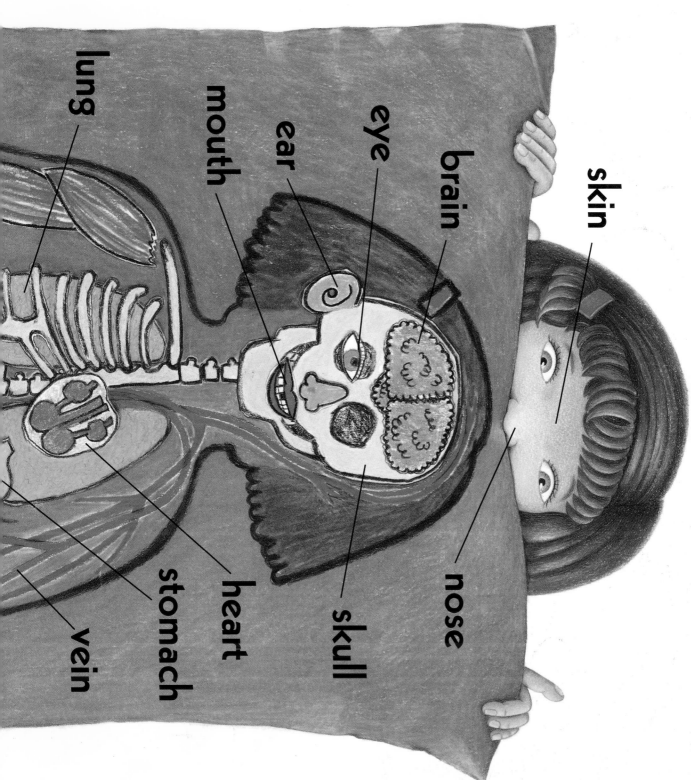

skin

brain

eye

ear

mouth

lung

nose

skull

heart

stomach

vein

. . . and keep me growing.
And someday I'll be all
grown up!
   Isn't it amazing?

And most amazing of all—every person in the world has a body that's very much the same, but every person is also very different.

There's no one else in the world exactly like you. And no one exactly like me.

Or ever will be!

AMAZING BODY FACTS

Your stomach digests about 2,190 quarts of food each year.
That's around 8,760 bowls of spaghetti!

Over half of your body's bones are in your hands and feet. That's more than 100 bones!

If you could line up all your blood vessels, they would wrap around the world *four* times!

When you sneeze, air comes out of your lungs at over 100 miles per hour!

Your brain weighs only about three pounds, but it can store billions of bits of information.

The heart beats around three billion times in an average person's life.

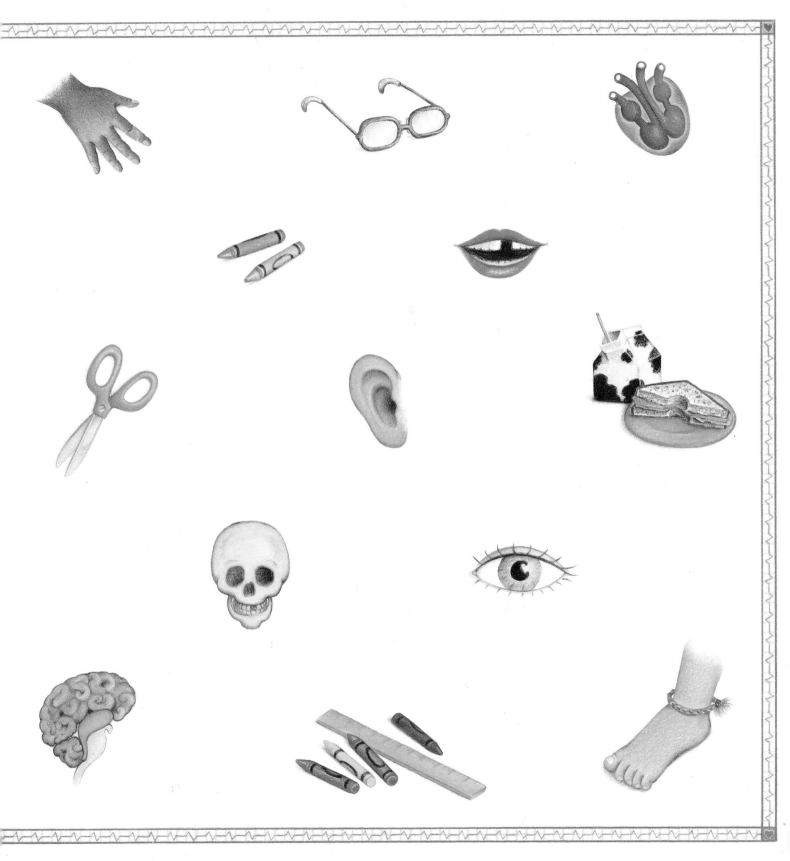

DEC 2 8 1999